The McNeill **Factor**

*How to Start and
Run a Successful
MasterMind Group*

ANN MCNEILL

ISBN 978-0-9837566-4-4

Library of Congress Control Number 2018951721

Published by

Emerge Publishing Group, LLC
Riviera Beach, FL
www.emergepublishers.com
561.601.0349

Ann McNeill 2018
The McNeill Factor

Printed in the United States of America

Table of Contents

Dedication

This book is dedicated to my husband, Daniel McNeill, who is the most important person in my life; My children: Danelle and Ionnie; My grandchildren: Malachi and Raja-Nia.

Acknowledgements

I would like to acknowledge:

My family,

The IMA Founders,

Fellow Master Minders,

MCO Construction Staff

National Association of Black Women in Construction,

Palm Beach Life Planners

And others too numerous to list

Foreword

Hold on!

You are getting ready to embark on the ride of your life. Within the pages of this book you will find a valuable tool that will teach you how to make your dreams a reality. It will show you how to daily use your skills and talents.

Ann McNeill is the definition of success. She discovered the secret years ago. Since then, she has helped multitudes discover the secret to a successful life.

Your success lies in your hands; however, Ann McNeill can help guide you through the process of developing and expressing your most powerful self. Ann is the master builder who builds stronger and better lives. Do not let this opportunity slip through your fingers.

As Ann so often says, "You must have a dream to make a dream come true." Are you ready to make your dreams come true? There is no guess-work involved. There is a proven system already in place to make things happen.

It is called *"The McNeill Factor."*

Les Brown
Motivational Speaker

My Story

On a brisk, cool night in December, reality slapped me in the face. It was New Year's Eve, 1980. I did not go out to enjoy the New Year's Eve festivities. Instead I stayed home, curled up on the sofa to enjoy a good book. That book was Napoleon Hill's *Think and Grow Rich* (TGR)nd it changed my life.

As a result of reading the book, I set a goal to save one-thousand dollars in the New Year, 1981. I had to have a plan to accomplish that goal. On that evening, I became aware that I was on a fast-track to nowhere financially. When I added up my income and my expenses, I realized my expenses exceeded my income.

How did I fall into this financial quagmire? Something had to give. Either my expenses had to be reduced or my income had to increase.

I began to read *Think and Grow Rich* and practice the principles. That book became my "bible" of sorts and like any religious zealot, I read it every day. I took it everywhere I went. I "preached" its principles to anybody who would listen. I gave the book to a small circle of friends at my local church in West

Palm Beach, and from there began to give the book as a gift for birthdays.

In *Think and Grow Rich,* I was introduced to the MasterMind concept of goal setting. Once I started to apply the principles in the book to my life, a paradigm shift took place. I began to move from mediocrity to excellence. I also realized it would be selfish to keep the MasterMind concept to myself. A large part of MasterMind is accountability, so I needed to share it with others. I needed a group of like-minded people to whom I would be accountable.

I began to meet in discussion groups with those to whom I had given the book. From this, the original MasterMind Women's Group was formed.

From that day to the present day, MasterMind has been a very important part of my life. My success in life is a direct result of MasterMinding. It is my hope that by implementing the system in this book and the accompanying workbook, it will have the same impact on you that it had on me.

This book, *The McNeill Factor,* will assist you in elevating your business or career to higher heights. Some of the people who benefitted from this system have shared testimonials that are interspersed throughout this book.

I wish you well as you take this new and exciting journey. Trust me. *The McNeill Factor* will work for you.

Ann McNeill

The Master Builder

CHAPTER 1

Introduction to MasterMinding

IN THIS CHAPTER
- What is a MasterMind Group?
- What a MasterMind Group is Not
- Napoleon's Hill Definition

At the writing of this book, I have been masterminding for thirty-seven years. The information in this book can be used by anyone who wants to move from mediocrity to excellence. Use these principles diligently and you will experience astounding results.

What is a MasterMind Group?

This is a group that offers a combination of brainstorming, education, peer accountability and support in a group to sharpen your business and personal skills. A mastermind group helps you and your mastermind group members achieve success. Group members challenge each other to set clear and concise goals, and more importantly, to accomplish them.

The first step in the mastermind process is to create a goal.

Next, formulate a plan to achieve it. Feedback from the group helps you with creative ideas and wise decision-making. During your mastermind meetings, you discuss your success stories as well as your challenges. Your group will applaud your success and help you solve your problems through peer brainstorming and collective, creative thinking.

What a MasterMind Group is NOT

It's not a class. During mid-year and annual conferences, the group can vote to bring in guest speakers. But the main focus of a mastermind group is the brainstorming and accountability support among the group members.

It's not group coaching. The feedback, advice and support are welcome from all group members. Success of the group is not contingent upon one person, facilitator, or coach. MasterMind groups are about the MEMBERS sharing with each other.

It's not a networking group. The main focus of the meeting is not sharing leads or resources with others. However, through connections with other members, you will find plenty of joint venture opportunities, lead sharing, and professional networking.

Napoleon's Hill Definition

In *Think and Grow Rich* by Napoleon Hill, the concept of the "master mind alliance" is introduced. The term has been shortened and modernized to "mastermind group." A direct quote of Napoleon Hill states, "The coordination of knowledge and effort of two or more people, who work toward a definite purpose, in the spirit of harmony."

Wafami MasterMind

I was first introduced to Think and Grow Rich by my mother. I was a teenager at the time. She would copy pages of the book and give them to me to read, highlighting portions that she wanted me to pay particular attention to because she knew I would have ignored it and chose instead to read novels by the likes of Terry McMillan, BeBe Moore Campbell and Eric Jerome Dickey. Before I even realized it, I had read the whole book!

So when I interviewed for a job with Ann McNeill in my early twenties and she asked during the interview if I had read *Think and Grow Rich*. My answer was a nonchalant, "I read that when I was 15." No need to mention how my mother tricked me into reading the book. Ann then introduced me to Ann McNeill's way of masterminding – daily affirmation, vision board, income circles, goals in ten areas (it was eight back then) of my life for one, five and ten years, accountability. This was not only new for me, it was foreign, but it was mandatory for my job. So there was really no choice. I had to plunge ahead into foreign territory.

I wrote my affirmation, set my goals with a deadline and began to review my goals and action plans weekly. I stumbled across my first mastermind report at the office earlier this year. I shouldn't have been, but I was surprised to see that the majority of those goals have been accomplished. I have published several books. I have lost weight (Gained it back. Now losing it again). I have grown spiritually. I've gotten married... Oh wait. That one hasn't happened yet. My bad.

One of my family goals was to start a mastermind group with my family. I would suggest it and they would ignore me. Finally, I guess light bulbs went off in their heads simultaneously, and they were ready to mastermind. We started Wafami MasterMind in 2008, and we have been masterminding as a family ever since. My sister and brother have gotten married and their spouses now mastermind too. Soon enough, my nieces and nephew will be masterminding also. They're two and three now. So we'll give them a year or two more.

MasterMinding has taught me how to set goals, focus on them and systematically track my progress. It helps me to see when I'm slacking and if something is really a goal. I am thankful that Ann introduced me to masterminding. It will definitely improve your life.

Kendy Ward

CHAPTER 2

Why MasterMind?

IN THIS CHAPTER

- 20 Reasons to MasterMind

There are many reasons to mastermind. Twenty reasons are listed here.

1. **Accountability**

   At the end of each meeting you will have an action plan, objectives you need to meet before the next meeting— which the group will hold you accountable for. Being held accountable by your mastermind partners ensures you maintain the disciplined behavior to succeed in your business.

2. **Establish new habits**

   A lot of your progress will be determined by the formation of new habits. Experience comes with patience and repetition. Only by eliminating or at least reducing old habits, and replacing them with positive new habits will you be allowed to grow personally and professionally.

3. Feedback

Receive feedback from successful individuals on how to solve business issues. If you have staff issues or financial challenges, let the mastermind group help you resolve them. Remember in the group we all have the same goal—to help each other grow their business or career. No hidden agendas—everyone is on the same page.

4. Perspective

It is hard to *be* yourself and *see* yourself at the same time. A mastermind group creates the space for you to step outside of your business or life and work *on* it rather than *in it*. Secondly, the diverse perspectives in the room will help you see opportunities where you may have had a blind spot. You will leave the group with new ideas and strategies for your business and life.

5. Brainstorming

Share your ideas and alternatives within your mastermind group. If you are not sure what to do next, what direction to go in, the collective power of the MasterMind will kick in and get you back on track.

6. Experience

In a mastermind group, you have access to collective wisdom. If there are 5 seasoned professionals in a group, you have access to 100 years of experience. These people come with diverse skill and subject mastery that you can tap into for free. That's why it is important to choose the right mastermind group.

7. Inspiration

It is contagious to see people around you grow. When you see them growing meeting after meeting, it will inspire your growth. When you were alone, seeing others grow may have made you jealous or insecure. But these are your teammates, and you know that they will share how they got that breakthrough with you and help you to get yours.

8. Helping Others

It was Zig Ziglar who said, "You can have everything in life you want if you will just help enough other people get what they want." You will get satisfaction from helping others.

9. Extend Your Network

Members of a MasterMind group all come with their own networks and over time they will usually share acquaintances as necessary. Every person in the mastermind group has an extended personal network and will be able to get introductions to many people they would otherwise never have access to.

10. Specific Knowledge

When discussing a specific topic it is very probable that one of the members will either have some knowledge on that subject or at least know whom to ask or where to find someone who can assist.

11. Relationships

Every person has four forms of their capital—their personal, intellectual, social, and financial capital. When you form a genuine mutual relationship with someone, you get access to all of their capital. Social capital is the multiplier and your mastermind group has already vetted hard working committed people like yourself and now you get to benefit from those relationships as a giver and receiver.

12. Energy

Members of a MasterMind group are developing a huge amount of new energy just by virtue of being part of a MasterMind group and getting all this awesome input. Once more this definitely has to do with the human nature of functioning best in a small, tightly knit group.

13. Leverage the Explainer Effect

When you have to explain a problem to someone else, often, the solution becomes evident to you as you are explaining the problem.

14. Resources

As with personal networks, every participant of a mastermind group will also have access to many resources that could benefit the entire group. If one can leverage these resources for the benefit of the group, the result often is even more augmented and the outcome becomes greater than the sum of the parts.

15. Support

Sometimes business is difficult and the challenge can seem overwhelming. Perhaps you have a difficult employee or a legal problem—chances are your mastermind colleagues have experienced the same issue. You will never be short of alternative suggestions on how to overcome issues. Additionally you will develop deep and meaningful friendships over and above all the business help.

16. Focus & Clarity

Sometimes the day to day activities of running a business or maintaining a challenging career can distract us. The mastermind group will keep you on track—just when you are losing focus, the group will remind you of your purpose and why you are in business.

17. Better Decision Making

It is easy to put off a decision—but with a mastermind group you have your own due-diligence team to give you the confidence you need when making an important decision.

18. Increased Confidence

Better decision making mean greater confidence—greater confidence spreads thorough your organization and inspires everyone to perform better. You will feel good. You will feel more confident.

19. Think bigger

You can't help but think bigger and stretch beyond your boundaries when surrounded by amazing people doing amazing things. Fellow mastermind members will help you to see the potential you are missing out on.

20. Creativity

This is one of the 10 areas we mastermind. If you are looking for new ideas for your business or if you want objective feedback and help with your new idea, the group will provide more ideas and constructive feedback on your ideas.

The above 20 benefits of a mastermind group are just a few of the many benefits. Having a mastermind group is like having your own personal team on deck at all times. Your team is ready to support your success the moment you say the word.

After you have been master minding for a time, you will be able to add more reasons to master mind to the above list.

A Student of Life

Testimony? Honestly, I think I am too young to have a testimony. Whenever I hear that word, I think of the days when I was younger and used to listen to the speeches of older people in church. So I think it is funny to even fathom the idea that I have a testimony, when some of them have had trials longer than I have been alive. For that reason I will call this my attestation regarding MasterMind.

Since I began as a child in MasterMind, I cannot honestly say that I know anything else, which would be life without goals and an action plan toward achieving those goals. As a result, my experience of a normal life is not other people's experience of typical life. I was always trying to use my time wisely, because I had no other choice. I was doing so many different things at the same time.

My goals and discipline were truly put on the test in high school, where I almost always made straight A's, took AP classes, played varsity basketball all four years, played varsity golf for 3 years, had my own business speaking to kids about investing, went to church every Sunday and Bible Study every Tuesday, taught a weekly youth investment class at my church for about 2 years, and with the rest of my time I ate and slept.

While going through it all, this was my mom, and at times I would think that I was doing too much because everyone around me was not doing as much. Even now looking back on it, it seems like a lot. But as I put it in perspective, I realize that everything I was doing could fit into one of the 9* areas that MasterMind encourages you to set goals in, and that in and of itself was balance.

Fortunately, during my first year of college I was not on track with my goals and was able to see the effect of not having goals in every area of my life. The experience was eye-opening. During my first semester the majority of my focus and time went to studying (education) and building my relationship with God (spiritual). But the concentration and overload in those areas led to misfortune in the others, such as health, personal, civic, and recreational.

After realizing how my life was out of whack and attending the end of the year MasterMind retreat, I started the New Year 2007 and the 2nd semester of my freshman year on a journey to get back on track. I wrote my goals more, began to take more time for myself, played intramural basketball and kept up my grades. In fact, I had all A's with a 19-credit load. Life was great, outstanding, amazing and I could feel the balance because I had peace.

Ionnie McNeill

*There are 10 areas now.

CHAPTER 3

Recruiting Members

IN THIS CHAPTER

- The Role of the Founding Members
- Who Can Be a Group Member
- Key Questions to Ask When Screening
  Potential Members

The Role of the Founding Members

The founding members set the standards for the group. As Ann McNeill's life transitioned over the years so did the group. For ten years, the group met every Saturday morning at 7:00 to discuss their goals, while experiencing tremendous growth in its membership. Every one of the founding members has a success story. MasterMinding literally changed their lives. It is their role to uplift and encourage others to take the mastermind path.

Who Can Be a Group Member?

When mastermind groups seek new members, they look for those individuals with like-minds. If this is not done, sooner, rather than later, the group will find that the person is not a good fit for their group. Groups have personalities. While one group may not be good for that person, there may be another group that is a perfect fit for that person.

Key Questions to Ask When Screening Potential Members

To get the most from your group you must be sure that all members you invite to your group meet specific requirements. To ensure the success of the group, each member must be a good fit. In order to do this, some hard questions must be asked of potential members.

These are crucial questions for screening members for your mastermind group:

1. What is Your Experience Level?

Find out if the others in this group are at a similar experience level to you. A step ahead or behind is acceptable, but more than that usually doesn't work out well for anyone.

Some examples: Is everyone in the group fresh out of college? Is everyone in the group 10-20 years into a career and they're starting a business on the side? Is this everyone's first business or just another in a portfolio of businesses?

2. When are You Available to Meet?

Make sure the people in your group are available when you're available. Since some meetings are via phone, ask about their time zone. It's not uncommon to meet someone at a conference, strike up a conversation, and not realize they live halfway around the world from you.

Ask them what days of week are ideal for a meeting of this kind. Make sure they can find a few days in their schedule so they can be flexible in case of scheduling conflicts that arise from time to time.

Find out what time of day they're thinking of having a mastermind call. Some people shut their brains off at 4:59 pm every day. Other people are night owls, and are ready to make progress in their business at midnight. This is something you need to know, up front, before you go any further.

3. Do You Have Time Available to Make Progress?

Make sure that all the members of the group have a similar expectation of how much time they can spend between meetings working toward their stated goals.

When someone commits to accomplishing a goal in a meeting, they must also have a corresponding pool of time in their lives set aside to work on those goals. If not, frustration quickly builds, week after week.

4. What is Your Business Model?

Successful mastermind groups have members that are all striving for common goals. Be mindful that not all mastermind groups focus on the same number of areas. Some may focus strictly on business. If so, make sure all the members of the business mastermind group are pursuing similar business models. As you will see from the survey, there are ten areas. Some groups may focus on five or six, while some groups only focus on business and finance.

For example, is your group comprised of eBook authors looking to achieve their first sale in the Kindle book store, or is it mostly freelance software developers looking to streamline client work?

While it's helpful to have a homogenous business model trend in the group, it can be beneficial when those members are in a variety of niches.

In a mastermind group of book authors, ask specific questions about the age level and genre of the books they're writing. All authors, differing niches.

In a mastermind group of freelance graphic designers, one can be a vector illustrator, one can be a UI/UX professional, another can be a specialist in banner ads, and another can be focused on posters and print media. All designers, different niches.

5. What is Your Revenue?

It's crucial that members in the group be of similar revenue levels. This is the #1 most difficult question to ask, but it's arguably the most important question of all.

Beginners who are still seeking their first dollar in their business shouldn't be matched with a business owner who has just passed the ten thousand a month mark growing his consulting business, and neither should be in a group with the founder of a company that is pulling in millions each year.

At every revenue level in business, there are hurdles and milestones. But those hurdles and milestones look different at each level.

To get the most out of any business-focused mastermind group, revenue levels must be fairly close among the members. This parity ensures that information flows in all directions in the meetings, and all members get their unique needs met most efficiently.

6. Do You Have a Day Job?

In the mastermind group, are they going to be discussing a side hustle, or their full-time business? We ask about day job to get an idea for the immovable time commitments in their lives.

If this is their primary job, are they a founder or co-founder in the business, or in an executive role where they can take the suggestions made in the group and apply them directly in their business?

If they're not in a role where they can effect change in your business, give this some extra thought. Non-founders can benefit from mastermind groups, for sure, but they shouldn't be mingled into a group with founders.

7. What Do You Need Help With Today?

Be sure to ask exactly what the prospective mastermind group member is hoping to receive from the group. Make sure what the person is looking for can actually be achieved in the group, and be sure their goals and needs are in alignment with the core strengths and weaknesses of the group and its members.

8. What Skills & Expertise Do You Bring to the Group?

In this question, you're turning the tables and asking what they're bringing into the group that can be of benefit to others. Every person in the mastermind group must be able and willing to help other members in some way.

This is crucial because no one is great at everything (despite what they may have you believe).

The ideal mastermind group contains a mix of people with complementary skills.

TESTIMONIAL

A Catalyst

On December 31, 2007 just minutes before the new year arrived, I declared publicly at Watch Night Service that 2008 would be the year of new beginnings. I fully believed that 2008 would bring major changes in my life. I did not know what kind of changes would take place, but I knew they would be positive and life-changing.

In January of 2008, Angela M. Williams, called me for a phone number. During the course of the conversation, she mentioned Professional Speakers Network (PSN), led by Dr. Tina Dupree. I joined and attended my first meeting in February. Ann McNeill, a former co-worker in corporate America, was there but had to leave early so I did not get a chance to speak with her.

The next month after the PSN meeting, Ann McNeil asked if I had read *Think and Grow Rich*. I had read the book 20 years earlier. Ann suggested I read it again. Of, course, she had a supply of them in the trunk of her car and gave me a copy. Ann proceeded to tell me about Master Mind and asked if I were interested. I was always interested in the master mind concept but never did anything about it. I was more than ready to join the group.

Two women (Ann and Angela) and two organizations (PSN and Master Mind) served as a catalyst that produced major changes in my life. I was evicted from the corridors of complacency.

As I focused on my speaking business, I was taught in the PSN meetings that all speakers need products for the back of the room (BOR) sales. When Angela spoke with me on that night in January, she informed me that over 70 members of PSN had written books. WOW! I decided that I would write a book before the end of 2008.

As I started to set goals in Master Mind, the vision became very clear .In April I formed Majestically Speaking. In May I formed Emerge Publishing Group, LLC. By September 13, 2008 I was having a book signing with not one, but two books hot off the press.

By December 13 of that same year, Emerge was hosting a book signing for another author. Who would have believed that by December 31, 2008, Emerge Publishing would have five finished products, three projects underway, and two more on the drawing board. This success has continued with other authors who have trusted Emerge Publishing with their masterpieces.

Over the two years, nine months that I have participated in master mind, I have seen those possibilities become reality. I know beyond the shadow of a doubt that working the master mind concept leads to guaranteed success. It does not matter about the level of education, or race or circumstances of birth. The fact that I was born in a shack on the edge of a bean-field in a migrant camp cannot and will not limit me.

It is so awesome that the bean-field baby has emerged into a board-room lady. I know that as I continue master minding and staying in the presence of God and the wonderful people that are a part of master mind, I will continue to reach unimaginable heights. I thank God for placing Ann McNeill and other goal-oriented, success-seeking individuals in my life.

Bettye Knighton
2010

CHAPTER 4

Group Leader Starter Kit

IN THIS CHAPTER

- Group Leader Responsibilities
- Starting A Group "Things To Do" check List
- Think & Grow Rich Questionnaire
- MasterMind Annual Survey
- Sample Meeting Agenda
- Sample Group Affirmation
- Sample Accountability Guidelines
- Sample Group Annual Report

Starting a Group "Things to Do" Check List				
Item	**Before Meeting #1**	**Meeting #1**	**Meeting #2**	**Meeting #3**
Identify prospective group members	√			
Open with prayer		√	√	√
Introductions		√	√	√
Choose group leader/coordinator		√		
History of MasterMind		√		
Discuss Think & Grow Rich (TGR)		√		
Requirement for participation		√		
Introduce MasterMind coach		√	√	√
Discuss development of new group		√		
Discuss benefits of workbook		√		
Homework – TGF questionnaire		√		
Homework—read 1st chapter of TGR		√		
Complete application and pay fee		√		
Set date for next meeting		√	√	√
Check homework from last meeting			√	√
Explain how to do affirmation			√	
Introduce concept of setting goals			√	
Explain how to use workbook			√	
Homework—write affirmation			√	
Homework—read 2ndchapter of TGR			√	
Spend time on MM process & workbook			√	√
Write annual goals for each area			√	√
Homework—read chapter 3 of TGR				√

The above chart is a sample of things to do for a new group. You may find other items that need to be accomplished to get your group off to a great beginning. Do not hesitate to make adjustments as necessary, but remember these items are tried and tested by some of the most effective MasterMind groups.

As you can see from the checklist, reading the *Think and Grow Rich* book is a very important part of the process. The information contained within *Think and Grow Rich* is timeless and priceless.

Think & Grow Rich Questionnaire

In the workbook that accompanies this text, you will find the questionnaire taken from Napoleon Hill's *Think & Grow Rich*. Space is allotted in the workbook for the answers. It is imperative that you complete this form prior to beginning your MasterMind journey. It will help you to begin to determine which goals you need to set. The questions are as follows:

1. Fix in your mind the exact amount of money you desire. It is not sufficient merely to say, "I want plenty of money." Be definite as to the amount. (There is a psychological reason for definiteness, which is described in *Think & Grow Rich*).

2. Determine exactly what products or services you intend to give for the money you desire. (There is no such reality as "something for nothing.")

3. Establish a definite date when you intend to possess the money you desire.

4. Create a definite plan for carrying out your desire, and begin at once, whether you are ready or not, to put this plan into action.

5. Write out a clear, concise statement of the amount of money you intend to acquire, name the time limit for its acquisition, state what you intend to give in return for the money, and describe clearly the plan through which you intend to accumulate it.

6. Read your written statement aloud, twice daily, once just before retiring at night, and once after arising in the morning. AS YOU READ, SEE, FEEL AND BELIEVE YOURSELF ALREADY IN POSSESSION OF THE MONEY.

Name::_____ Phone:_____ Email:_____

SURVEY: A PERSONAL ASSESSMENT

THE FUNDAMENTALS OF THE SURVEY

The survey is completed at the beginning of each year. The survey will assist you in setting your goals for the year. It is beneficial to complete the survey prior to setting your goals each year.

The survey is to be completed and included in your report. Completing the survey before writing your goals helps you define goals in each area of your life. This is because the survey gives you an overview of where balance is needed. If you notice a lot of "no's" in the area of health, then you know you are out of balance in that area and need to set goals in order to achieve stability, and continued growth and happiness.

THE TEN AREAS OF YOUR LIFE

Remember the annual survey is the starting point to help you grow and reflect on important areas of your life. Be truthful and upfront with yourself.

1. SPIRITUAL
Humans are triune beings. The three parts of our being are body, mind and spirit. To become balanced individuals we must not neglect our spirits

2. FAMILY
Family is an area sometimes overlooked or not thought of at all. This normally happens because in our minds we take for granted that by default they are automatically first. It is important that we have very definitive family goals and aspirations.

3. FINANCIAL
A great deal of the stress that a lot of us encounter is because of mismanagement of finances. This exercise helps us to place everything in our lives into perspective.

4. HEALTH
We have only one body and when it is ruined that is it. We do not get another one. So it would be in our best interest to take care of our bodies.

5. EDUCATIONAL
Knowledge is power and we are on an eternal quest for knowledge. Acquiring knowledge is how we grow as individuals.

6. PERSONAL DEVELOPMENT
Personal goals are set to remind us that we have to invest time in ourselves.

7. BUSINESS/CAREER
In your business or career, you should have definite goals. The setting and achieving of these goals can be the measure of your growth in business or your career.

8. RECREATIONAL
Many times we let the other areas of our lives crowd in on us, and we forget to take a moment to enjoy life. Sometimes we need a recess from our lives, a moment to just laugh, have fun and live.

9. CIVIC
This is relative to your community involvement. As citizens we all have an obligation to give back to others what we have learned so that we can help fuel the next generation.

10. CREATIVITY
We all have innate creative qualities which are often revealed in subjects that capture our interest. For many, creativity comes naturally and is hard to deny. For others, self discovery, reflections, or perhaps a classroom setting may be utilized to reveal and fine tune hidden talents.

On the next page you will see a sample of the survey that is in your workbook.

SURVEY: A PERSONAL ASSESSMENT

SPIRITUAL

	DATE		DATE		DATE		COMMENTS / NOTES
	YES	NO	YES	NO	YES	NO	
Do you read your Bible daily/weekly?							
Do you give to worthwhile causes?							
Do you attend services to receive spiritual growth?							
Is your spiritual life balanced?							
Do you include your family in your spiritual plans?							
Do you do something to make this world a better place spiritually?							
Have you planned your faith period?							
Do you meditate?							
Do you believe in a Creator?							
Are you helping others?							

FAMILY

	DATE		DATE		DATE		COMMENTS / NOTES
	YES	NO	YES	NO	YES	NO	
Do you have a Family Mission Statement?							
Do you have Family Time (monthly/weekly)?							
Do you make time to spend with your siblings?							
Are all family members insured?							
Are you helping family members to set goals and make plans?							

A PERSONAL ASSESSMENT

FINANCIAL

	DATE		DATE		DATE		COMMENTS / NOTES
	YES	NO	YES	NO	YES	NO	
How much money do you want? $_____							
Are you current in filing your taxes?							
Do you know how much money you need to retire?							
Have you maxed out your 401K?							
Have you maxed out your Tax Shelter Annuity?							
if Self-Employed have you maxed out your SEP/Single K?							
Have you maxed out your Individual Retirement Account?							
Have you maxed out your Roth IRA?							
Do you have Long-term savings?							
Do you have Short-term savings?							
Do you invest in stocks?							
DRIPS (Dividend Reinvestment Plan)?							
Do You have Car Insurance?							
Do You have Homeowners' Insurance?							
Do You have Life Insurance on self and family members?							
Do you have Disability Insurance?							
Do you have Long Term Care Insurance?							
Do you have an updated Will?							
Do you utilize a Trust in your estate plan?							
Does your family know where you keep important papers?							
Are you a member of Better Investing?							
Have you checked your credit score this year?							
Are you a homeowner?							
Do you own Investment property?							

SURVEY: A PERSONAL ASSESSMENT

HEALTH

	DATE	YES	NO	DATE	YES	NO	DATE	YES	NO	COMMENTS / NOTES
Have you had a:										
WOMEN: Annual PAP Exam?										
MEN: Prostate Exam?										
GENERAL HEALTH (Have you received these exams?)										
Colonic exam?										
Eye exam?										
Dental exam/ dental cleaning twice yearly?										
Breast exam?										
Colonoscopy?										
Heart Disease exam?										
Bone Density exam?										
Podiatry?										
Do you have a Primary Care Physician?										
Do you have health insurance?										

EDUCATION

	DATE	YES	NO	DATE	YES	NO	COMMENTS / NOTES
Continued Education?							
No. of books Read Annually?							
Are your children going to college?							
Do you have a daily time to study?							
Will you share your knowledge with others?							
Do you possess education balance?							
Are you going to achieve great wisdom?							

SURVEY: A PERSONAL ASSESSMENT

PERSONAL DEVELOPMENT

	DATE		DATE		DATE		COMMENTS / NOTES
	YES	NO	YES	NO	YES	NO	
Do you have a specific activity for Personal Development?							
Do you set goals for:							
6 months?							
1 year?							
5 years?							
10 years?							
29 years?							

BUSINESS & CAREER

	DATE		DATE		DATE		COMMENTS / NOTES
	YES	NO	YES	NO	YES	NO	
Do you own a business?							
Do you have a business plan of action?							
Do you have a financial plan/forecast for your business?							
Do you have prearranged plan to sell/liquidate business at your:							
Death?							
Disability?							
Retirement?							
Are key people insured in the event of death or disability?							
Have you paid quarterly taxes (941)?							
Is your employee compensation package competitive?							
Have you set up a Dun & Bradstreet # for your business?							
Do you set regular appointments to market your business?							

SURVEY: A PERSONAL ASSESSMENT

RECREATION

	DATE		DATE		DATE		COMMENTS / NOTES
	YES	NO	YES	NO	YES	NO	
Do you travel for fun and recreation?							
Do you take a vacation?							
Do you have a personal fitness program?							
Do you plan time for family recreation?							
Are you living a recreationally balanced life?							
Do you plan to take time off for yourself?							

CIVIC (ASSOCIATIONS)

	DATE		DATE		DATE		COMMENTS / NOTES
	YES	NO	YES	NO	YES	NO	
Are you a member of any Professional Organizations?							
Are you a member of any Spiritual Organizations?							
Are you a member of any Volunteer/Non-Profit Organizations?							
Are you a member of any Social Organizations?							

CREATIVITY

	DATE		DATE		DATE		COMMENTS / NOTES
	YES	NO	YES	NO	YES	NO	
Do you have a hobby or collect and display items?							
Do you have a talent and an opportunity to share it with others?							
Are you inspired by art and exhibits?							
Have you ever thought of writing a book?							

TESTIMONIAL

Walking the Walk

Ann McNeill has been phenomenal at the mastermind process. One of the things that a person can appreciate about an instructor, teacher or coach is them having walked the walk. Ann shares her experience with others so that they can be liberated and free.

When she talks about desire and specialized knowledge, she knows what she is talking about because she has been there. I really appreciate her vulnerability and the gifts she gives to other. She is an amazing woman.

John Register

TESTIMONIAL

Change Agent

Through Ann McNeill, I was introduced to the mastermind process. My life has changed dramatically since I met her in so many ways. She has brought exposure to the MasterMind process. Ann McNeill is truly the Master Builder.

Shirley Burke

Sample Agenda - First Group Meeting

Date: _____ Time: _____ Location: _____

I. Call to order and Prayer/Meditation

II. Introductions by everyone

III. Advisor goes over information on these pages, answering any questions
   a. History and Founder
   b. Why MasterMind?
   c. Member Code Ethics and Member Policies (Accountability)

IV. The Advisor will discuss the roles members may take within the group
   a. Group Leader, Chaplain, Secretary, Assistant to any of these if group prefers
   b. Group will decide on Group Leader

V.   Agree on weekly "coaching" call dates with Advisor for next eight weeks (e.g. Thursdays, 7p-8p)

VI. Decide on a group name

VII. Set the date for the next group face-to-face meeting

VIII. Any wrap up discussion

IX. Closing Prayer/Meditation and Adjournment

Sample Agenda - Second Group Meeting

Date: _____ Time: _____ Location: _____

I.   Call to Order and Opening Prayer/Meditation

II.   Recite Member Code of Ethics in unison

III. Discuss and Submit completed/signed documents to Group Leader with copies
      a. Self-Contract
      b. Annual Survey

IV.   With MasterMind Group Advisor
      a. Review how to use the MasterMind Workbook
      b. Complete the *Think and Grow Rich* Questionnaire
      c. Discuss MM affirmation and personal affirmation

V.   Discuss/Finalize

a. Meeting dates, locations, time options, including next meeting

b. Attendance policy Agreement to be used by group

c. Accountability Guidelines and Acknowledgments to be used by the group

VI.   Discuss completed reading assignment for *Think and Grow Rich.*

VII. Agree on reading schedule for the rest of the *Think and Grow Rich* book or follow the suggested schedule included in these pages.

VIII. Confirm Homework due next meeting

a. As assigned by master mind group advisor

b. *Think and Grow Rich* reading assignment from agreedupon schedule.

IX.   Closing Prayer/Meditation and Adjournment

Sample Agenda - Third Group Meeting

Date: _____ Time: _____ Location: _____

I.   Call to Order and Opening Prayer/Meditation

II. Recite Member Code of Ethics in unison

III. Discuss and Submit completed/signed documents to Group Leader with copies
   a. Signed Group Attendance Agreement
   b. Signed Group Accountability Guidelines and Acknowledgment

IV. Discuss completed *Think and Grow Rich* reading assignment

V.   Discuss each member's finalized goals and personal affirmation

VI.   Discuss Income circles   (You will find these in the workbook)

VII. Discuss the master mind booklist and decide which books the group will read for the rest of year

VIII. Confirm next meeting date/time/location from agreed upon schedule

IX.   Confirm next scheduled reading assignment

X.   Adjourn with closing prayer/meditation

Once the group has met three times, the *Standard Agenda* will be used. Even the meetings via phone will follow the standard agenda. This keeps the group focused and on task. Productive people are busy people, therefore, time should be spent judiciously. That is why an agenda is so important.

Sample Standard Agenda - MasterMind Group Meeting

Date: _____ Time: _____ Location: _____

I. Call to Order and Opening prayer/meditation

II. Recite group affirmation

III. Make any reports as needed (e.g. if member assigned project, task; report progress here)

IV. Read personal affirmation

V. Share progress on action plans for goals since last meeting (discuss challenges, solutions as needed)

VI. Finalize any discussions from previous meeting as appropriate

VII.   Discuss any business

    a. Group Leader Report

    b. MM upcoming events (e.g. Mid-Year, Annual conference, etc.)

VIII. Discuss completed reading assignment

IX.   Confirm next scheduled reading assignment and next meeting date/time/location

X.   Adjourn with closing prayer/meditation

Group Leader: Tips for Running Effective Meetings

✓ Make sure you have everything you will need for the upcoming meeting

✓ Confirm meeting logistics with all attendees

✓ Circulate an agenda to all attendees at least 24 hours before meeting date/time

    o Agenda should indicate meeting time limit

    o Suggestion: indicate time limit for each agenda item such as reports, discussions

    o Make sure agenda items are listed in order of priority

✓ Start and end the meeting at the agreed upon time

✓ Keep the meeting moving by

    o Following the agenda

    o Redirecting off-topic discussions back to agenda topics

    o Staying within established time limits for each agenda item

Note: **While the individual's report is being given, we, as a group, will not interject questions or comments. All questions/**

comments will be written down and addressed upon the conclusion of that person's report.

TESTIMONIAL

Growth

Over twenty-eight years ago my prayer partner and friend, Ann McNeill, not only suggested I read *Think and Grow Rich,* she gave me a copy of it. I didn't immediately read the book. I did eventually get around to reading it and found it very thought provoking. Every time we talked she would share with me what she was doing in her life, and what new inspirational book she was reading. She would inquire about my goals and what I was doing to reach them. Then she would encourage me to achieve my goals. As a result I read *Success: The Glenn Bland Method* and *The University of Success.* Little did I know that we were "masterminding" at the time.

Over the years, Ann and I continued to have our talks. I was not participating in the MasterMind group, which by now was growing, but she was having her own private sessions with me. As a person I have grown tremendously. I am able to cross of my list of goals which were set and have been accomplished, I am usually reading 3-4 books at a time, which are motivational, inspirational and informational. I have devoted more time to recreational activities and feel that my life is more balanced. I Have also written two books.

One of my goals is to never stop masterminding, no matter where I am or what I am doing. As long as I have some means of communication, I can mastermind with someone. I thank Ann for not being selfish and not keeping all of what she learned to herself. Her willingness to share this knowledge has helped so many to change the direction of their lives and to live a fruitful and balanced life.

Lynn Whitfield

Sample Group Affirmation

We are a group where we can continually grow spiritually, mentally, physically, financially, health wise, family wise and in business.

We value honesty, integrity, and abundance in ourselves and in others.

We create an environment where each of us can find support and encouragement in achieving our life's goals.

We maintain patience through understanding.

We always resolve conflicts with each other rather than harboring anger.

We wisely use our time, talents and resources to bless others.

Our group is happy and prosperous and we have fun together.

We support each other fully in our seen and unseen potential by showing unconditional love and inspiration for each other.

We discuss all aspects of life.

We serve each other and the community.

We plan our work and we work our plan.

We believe all things are possible through Christ who strengthens us.

We plan to leave a legacy of strength and importance of seeking first the kingdom while growing individually and collectively.

Sample Accountability Guideline

1. Individual monthly and quarterly goals are submitted to the group on the deadlines set by the group. There are no grace periods unless agreed upon by a majority of the group on a case by case basis.

2. Members agree to meet weekly in person (or via telephone) as agreed to by the majority of the group members. Meetings will begin promptly at the agreed upon time and last approximately one and one-half hours. Repeated tardiness will not be condoned and could result in removal from the group.

3. Goals submitted should be specific, measurable, and verifiable.

4. Members should try to make goals that are attainable and MUST, no exceptions, submit one goal per month for the first three months, quarterly goals to be added beginning month four. With a reasonable excuse, a member will be excused one time, receive a warning the second time and the third time will be asked to leave the group due to lack of commitment.

5. If a member feels the need to drop or make changes that reduce the outcome of the monthly or quarterly goal(s), they must discuss it with the group to get clarity regarding the block that is occurring. Penalties may be added at a later date. Monthly and quarterly goals are reported on at the group meetings. Failure to complete goals over three consecutive months will result in being asked to leave the group.

6. If a member leaves the group at any time, for any reason, he/she agrees to forfeit his/her spot in the group.

7. Confidentiality – As members share specifics of their businesses and personal lives, these matters are confidential and not to be shared with anyone outside of the group without written permission from the affected party.

8. A new group member may be proposed and admitted upon a majority vote of all existing members. The perspective member shall visit the group three times to fulfill a probationary period. The vote will be cast via written secret ballot.

9. A member may be recommended for dismissal from the group. This could be based on a member's not adhering to critical issues, not adhering to the rules set forth, not setting

appropriate goals, not contributing to the group's learning experience or any other issue that does not advance the learning of the group. At that point, that member will be voted on by secret ballot. It is found that the member does not fit in with the group any longer, upon a majority vote, he/she will be asked to leave.

_____   _____
Date   Signature

Master Mind Group Reporting Form

Annual Reporting Form

Name of MasterMind Group	Date Established

Name of Person Providing Report:

Date Completed:

General Information

Type of Group:	Adult	Youth

Name of Group Leader:

Number of Members	
Frequency of Meeting	
Type of Meeting	

Greatest Accomplishments Last Month

One rose (something good):

One thorn (roadblock):

One major lesson learned on behalf of the group:

TESTIMONIAL

Cause and Effect

I knew I needed to fix me. Talking to others made me feel good at times, but rarely did it move me out of my place of ineffectiveness for very long. I found reading to be the most effective way for me to access and gather information. I could do this no matter where I was in the world.

Over the years, I have compiled a vast library of good books. But the group of books that made the difference for me, told me that magic did not exist and the only way to move forward from where I was, to where I wanted to be, was to actively train my ability to FOCUS my THOUGHTS, VISUALIZE my DESIRED DESTINY, and move forward with a SPECIFIC PLAN, supported by DELIBERATE ACTIONS attacking ONE GOAL AT A TIME.

When this state of mind is achieved, the people who have been waiting to assist you will gladly spring into action to support your vision. Your vision and activity will create mutual, respectful, spiritual, and economic opportunity for all who will come in contact with it. The MASTER MIND philosophy and organization is the way for men and women to deliberately succeed at everything they desire to achieve. If I can do it, I know you can too. What do you have to lose? Only the position you are presently in…and you don't want to be there anyway!

The Master Mind System has provided me with a unique way of looking at my ideas, vision, and problems, Through the Master Mind system, I have discovered the system of setting goals, creating action plans, systematically hand selecting a master mind alliance which is my goal-specific team and accountability system. I have tried to work with groups using other systems and they have shown themselves to be ineffective and usually rapidly degenerated into social groups or just disbanded completely. The Master Mind system is a complete philosophy that has been used at the highest levels of our government, business and industry, and in your personal life informally. If you would like to make progress on a day to day basis and maintain a well-rounded life, Master Mind is the way to go.

Ann McNeill, my mother would smack me in the head if I did not give honor, to whom honor is due. Honor is due to you. Your vision and your example has a breath of fresh air for the Black man. It is rare that you get to associate with a real successful person who allows you to touch them and they touch you back. I thank you for ALL you have poured into my life and as I pay it forward, I give great honor to you for

I did what you said and I sold the principal of my school on an appointment. Now I am going to offer my services, and ask for a recommendation to his principal friends along with the County wide principal network. I will keep you posted. You have helped to save another life and changed the future for the nations that will spring forward from me.

Rufus Curry, Jr.

CHAPTER 5

How It Works

IN THIS CHAPTER
- Setting SMART Goals
- Weekly Reporting

Setting SMART Goals

The group has been formed. The members have been selected. Now what?

How does the McNeill Factor work? What are the steps? The key to the system is setting SMART goals:

S = specific

M = measurable

A = attainable

R = realistic

T = time

The very first step is setting goals following the above standards. In the meetings, goals are discussed. Each week the members share goals that they want to be held accountable for that week. No one wants to show up week after week with the same goals because this indicates the member has not been diligent in meeting his/her goals.

Weekly Reporting

To help trace goals, actions, milestones, a Weekly Report form is shown on the next page. In the accompanying workbook, there are complete sets of weekly reports. More copies can be made if needed. The weekly report consists of the ten areas that the McNeill Factor recommends: They are: Spiritual, Personal, Health, Family, Financial, Business/Career, Educational, Recreational, Civic and Creativity. This is a comprehensive list. It is perfectly acceptable to focus on a select few; but remember, this list provides balance.

When a goal is set and met, that is success. Following this system consistently is guaranteed to produce great results.

On the pages that follow is the key to *The McNeill Factor.* Do these pages diligently and you will begin to experience astounding results.

WEEKLY MASTERMIND PLAN

NAME: _____

FOR WEEK OF: _____

MEMORY SCRIPTURE or QUOTE FOR THE MONTH:

SPIRITUAL GOALS:	Accomplished

Book:	Pgs.	Projected		Pgs.	Actual

SPIRITUAL GOALS ACTION PLAN:	M	T	W	T	F	S	S	%

FAMILY GOALS:						Accomplished	

Book:	Pgs.	Projected		Pgs.	Actual

FAMILY GOALS ACTION PLAN:	M	T	W	T	F	S	S	%

FINANCIAL GOALS:						Accomplished	

Book:	Pgs.	Projected		Pgs.	Actual

FINANCIAL GOALS ACTION PLAN:	M	T	W	T	F	S	S	%

HEALTH GOALS:					Accomplished			

Book:	Pgs.	Projected		Pgs.	Actual			

HEALTH GOALS ACTION PLAN:	M	T	W	T	F	S	S	%

EDUCATIONAL GOALS:					Accomplished			

Book:	Pgs.	Projected		Pgs.	Actual			

EDUCATIONAL GOALS ACTION PLAN:	M	T	W	T	F	S	S	%

PERSONAL GOALS:							**Accomplished**		

Book:	Pgs.	Projected		Pgs.	Actual

PERSONAL GOALS ACTION PLAN:	M	T	W	T	F	S	S	%

BUSINESS/CAREER GOALS:							**Accomplished**		

Book:	Pgs.	Projected		Pgs.	Actual

BUSINESS/CAREER GOALS ACTION PLAN:	M	T	W	T	F	S	S	%

RECREATIONAL GOALS:	Accomplished

Book:	Pgs.	Projected	Pgs.	Actual

RECREATIONAL GOALS ACTION PLAN:	M	T	W	T	F	S	S	%

CIVIC GOALS:	Accomplished

Book:	Pgs.	Projected	Pgs.	Actual

CIVIC GOALS ACTION PLAN:	M	T	W	T	F	S	S	%

CREATIVITY GOALS:					**Accomplished**		

Book:							
	Pgs.	Projected		Pgs.	Actual		

CREATIVITY GOALS ACTION PLAN:	M	T	W	T	F	S	S	%

This week's meeting place: _____ Date:_____

Attendees:

    1. _____   4._____

    2. _____   5._____

    3. _____   6._____

Next week's meeting place:_____ Date:_____

Notes:

TESTIMONIAL

Destiny Helpers

By immersing herself in the Think and Grow Rich philosophy, Ann McNeill is fast emerging as a "Destiny Helper" assisting people to stretch their mental and spiritual being to achieve their God-given purpose and still operate in wholeness.

My education and career path taught me how to develop goals, objectives and specific tasks to achieve the goals and objectives. I had become a list maker, very confined and defined. Everything I did I understood and it all made sense.

One day I made the mistake of verbalizing this to Ann and she promptly expressed the following McNeillism: "There is the problem. You are working a process that makes 'CENTS' and you should be opening your mind to the Think and Grow Rich Philosophy so you can make "DOLLARS."

Sharon Jackson

CHAPTER 6

The Beginning

IN THIS CHAPTER
- The Vision
- A Fresh Start

The Vision

My vision is to encourage the spirit of self-help with accountability for individuals and organizations to help create a better quality in life and business.

A Fresh Start

You have made some important steps. The first step was to purchase this book and the accompanying workbook. Everything you need to know to be successful is in the book. The workbook has the annual survey, the income circles the sample affirmations. Whatever you need is there.

It is time to establish new habits that will propel you to reach higher heights. The Workbook contains several sets of Weekly Report forms that are shown in this book. Use these diligently. Each area we mastermind has a goal section and plan of action section. It is not sufficient to set goals; you MUST have a plan of action.

Do not be concerned about the failures of the past. This is a new day and you are making a fresh start. When practiced diligently, the McNeill Factor system will work for you. You will experience metamorphosis.

Remember, you must have a dream to make a dream come true!

Metamorphosis

I have been a member of the Master Mind group since 1990, and it has changed my life tremendously. I started out being totally dependent upon others to make things happen for me and my children. I had very low self-esteem, no desire to do more than necessary, and I believed that everyone owed me something.

This road was taking me nowhere fast as a single mom living with my mother. Ann was my mom's best friend and she saw the destructive road I was headed down so she set out to help me see myself and my future in a new light. The first thing to be done was to begin to build my self-confidence and change my mindset. This was no easy task. To say the least, I was very stubborn and hard to communicate with because I thought I knew all the answers. It is important that my past is understood in order for my present to be appreciated.

I started my journey by reading my first book outside of my school text books called *Think and Grow Rich* by Napoleon Hill. Upon completion of this book there are 6 questions in the book that I had to answer. Those questions were the wake-up call that I needed in order to become the success that I now knew I could be. The short version of my story is that once I began to see myself in a different light through Master Mind my life changed tremendously.

I added balance to my life. Today I am a successful business woman. My daughters are also master minders, and are both using the principles in their lives. I encourage you to become a member of a Master Mind group. It will be the most important change you will ever make in your life. Remember, keep reading!

Nifretta Thomas

About the Author

Ann McNeill is a proud graduate of Florida Memorial University. She is the founder and former president of the International MasterMind Association For more than thirty-seven years she has partnered with other master minders to support one another for success. She has developed a system called the McNeill Factor that has been responsible for the success of many people.

Ann McNeill is also the Founder of MCO Construction & Services, Inc., a full service construction company dedicated to delivering projects on time, within budget, and in compliance with the special needs of large public and private projects. MCO has performed construction with a combined value in excess of $110 million. In an industry with few black or female run companies, MCO Construction is a stand-out example of possibilities. *MCO is a small company with a large presence.*

Ann formed the *National Association of Black Women in Construction* (NABWIC), which provides, education and support for the contractors.

Ann McNeill is an innovative community activist, a pioneer in the field of youth and adult investment clubs for African Americans, a noted speaker, and a proud wife, mother and grandmother. Her career has been built one challenge and one opportunity at a time.

For more information please contact:

The McNeill Factor

1450 North Mangonia drive

West Palm Beach, Florida 33401

Phone: 786-546-0184

Email: annmcneill03@yahoo.com

www.ingramcontent.com/pod-product-compliance
Lightning Source LLC
Chambersburg PA
CBHW072223170526
45158CB00002BA/725

* 9 7 8 0 9 8 3 7 5 6 6 4 4 *